champagne

Neil Mathieson

PRC

Previous page: Moët & Chandon's Dom Perignon: probably the world's best known champagne.

This edition first published in 1999 by
PRC Publishing Ltd,
Kiln House, 210 New Kings Road, London SW6 4NZ

Copyright © 1999 PRC Publishing Ltd.

All rights reserved. No part of this publication may
be reproduced, stored in a retrieval system, or
transmitted in any form or by any means, electronic, mechanical,
photocopying, recording, or otherwise, without the prior written
permission of the Publisher and copyright holders.

ISBN 1 85648 521 8

Printed and bound in Hong Kong

Glossary

Assemblage	The blending of the wines
B.O.B.	Buyer's Own Blend
C.I.B.	Champagne Information Bureau
C.I.V.C.	Comité Interprofessionnel du Vin de Champagne
Cuvée	the term used for the first pressing and a final blend
Dégorgement	the elimination of sediment following the second fermentation
Gyropallate	metal cage for automatic riddling
Hectare	land measurement of 10,000 square metres or approximately 2.47 acres.
Pupitre	the wooden bottle racks used during remuage
Remuage	the oscillation and tilting of the bottles to send the sediment from second fermentation in to the neck of the bottle
Tailles	the second pressings of the grapes

Written by Neil Mathieson, Managing Director of Eaux de Vie Ltd, the U.K.'s leading independent spirit shipper and importer of Champagne.

Acknowledgements

Thanks to all the Champagne houses who have helped in the research. Particular thanks go to Tim Banks of the C.I.B. in London and Phillipe Le Tixerant, lately with the C.I.V.C. in Épernay, and his greeting of 'you again' when greeting me at his offices for the third time in two months. To the various U.K. trade publications such as *Harpers Wine & Spirit Gazette* and *Wine & Spirit International* who have kept me up to date with the latest happenings in the Champagne region and also to all those who supplied information, labels, pictures — in particular the Champagne Information Bureau in London — for providing many of the pictures and of, course, the many samples provided for photography and tasting.

    Additional information has been gathered over twenty-five years of discussion, tasting and many visits to the area where the unfailing generosity of one's host never fails to match the brilliance of the product. To cold mornings in frosty vineyards, deafening technical sessions in bottling and disgorging halls and to the samples and advice, both willingly supplied by my many colleagues in the wine trade.

Contents

INTRODUCTION 4
   The History 4
   The Champagne Region 6
   The Vineyards and the Vines 8
   Wine Production 10
   Types of Wine 12
   Buying, Storing, and Serving
      Sparkling Wines 14
   The Bottle 15
THE WINES 16
   Beaumet 18
   Billecart-Salmon 20
   Boizel 22
   Bollinger 24
   F. Bonnet 26
   Canard-Duchêne 28
   de Castellane 30
   Charles de Cazanove 32
   Guy Charbaut 34
   Veuve Clicquot-Ponsardin 36
   Cordornìu 38
   Deutz 40
   Devaux 42
   Domain Chandon 44
   Duval-Leroy 46
   Nicolas Feuillatte 48
   Freixenet 50
   Gosset 52
   Heidsieck & Co. Monopole 54
   Charles Heidsieck 56
   Jacquart 58
   Krug 60
   Charles Lafitte 62
   Lanson 64
   Laurent-Perrier 66
   Lindauer and Deutz 68
   Mercier 70
   Moët & Chandon 72
   G. H. Mumm 74
   Mumm Cuvé Napa 76
   Perrier-Jouët 78
   Philipponat 80
   Piper-Heidsieck 82
   Pommery 84
   Louis Roederer 86
   Pol Roger 88
   Ruinart 90
   Seppelt Great Western 92
   Taittinger 94

FURTHER READING 96

champagne

Introduction

THE HISTORY

Wine has been produced in the Champagne region for centuries. In the distant past it was mostly still, red, table wine, whose popularity over the years probably owed more to the vineyards' close proximity to Paris than any claim to superior quality. From the Roman Empire to the current day, therefore, champagne has been popular, asked for by name and drunk by kings — but the type of wine we now know as champagne was not developed until the late 17th century. Then it was noticed that the unintentional sparkle the wine had in some years could be captured and fewer bottles would be lost in the spring when the temperatures rose leading to the secondary fermentation of that yeast left over from the first fermentation.

It was during this century that the legendary monks and landowners of the area developed the skills and techniques that give us the champagne we now enjoy. The monk Dom Perignon, from 1668 cellarer at the Benedictine Abbey at Hautvillers, was foremost of the wine-makers at that time, and he is widely credited with showing other wine-makers the benefits of judicious blending, producing clean white wines from red grapes, and of using good quality cork closures to capture the resultant sparkling wine. His work was greatly advanced by the Brularts of Sillery and Nicholas Ruinart, nephew of Dom Ruinart, a contemporary of Dom Perignon. By the end of the century, such was the reputation of the quality of the wines from Champagne that the English and French royal courts had taken a great liking to them and the business was becoming much more profitable.

In the early 1700s, the first champagne houses were opening: fortunately for all of us

introduction

Claude Moët's was one of them. No one from the region can possibly deny the influence this famous name has had on the champagne industry as it grew up. Claude Moët, his son Claude-Louis, and Claude-Louis's son, Jean-Remy Moët, were pivotal in establishing supply lines with the growers, developing export markets, and securing the fame of the wines. By the early 1800s the Moëts' friendship with Napoleon had secured vital patronage and by the late 1800s the company — now called Moët & Chandon — was by far the biggest landowner in the area and was selling more than two million bottles every year!

Later in the 1800s other famous names appeared and, despite the hardships of two world wars this century, most of these famous houses remained family concerns until international financiers moved in during the 1960s. Even more consolidation has taken place during the late 1990s and, as this book goes to

Below: The man himself — Dom Perignon (1635-1718) cellarer at the abbey of Hautvillers, whose vineyards are now owned by Moët & Chandon.

press, great names such as Perrier Jouët, G.H. Mumm, and de Venoge are changing hands for figures far higher than the humble monk, Dom Perignon, could ever have dreamed.

Champagne and Sparking wines

Here, we will confine ourselves to the finest of sparkling wines, those made by what is known as the *Méthode Champenoise* or the traditional method. This was probably first instigated by the followers of Dom Pérignon at the turn of the 18th century, but was certainly aided in its development by the many experiments conducted by winemakers around the world. It was not until the mid-1800s that a full understanding of the functions of the sugars and yeasts in the *liqueur de tirage* became common knowledge, and the effervescence within the wine was controlled properly. From then onwards the future of the previously undesired fizz was secure.

Good sparkling wine is now made in all wine producing areas but the simple history is best left to the Champenois to tell, although should the current development of high quality wines continue, especially in the New World, then they will have to look to their laurels.

THE CHAMPAGNE REGION

The region of Champagne in the north-west of France is made up of the four départements of Ardennes, Marne, Aube, and Haut-Marne, and has been firmly part of France since 1285, when Jeanne, heiress of Champagne, married Philip, heir to the French throne. Although almost the size of Belgium, the region's wines are now produced within a delimited area in a small range of hills centered on the Marne River, some 100 miles (150km) from Paris.

There are four major vineyard areas situated within the Marne and Aube départements; three around Reims and Epernay, and the fourth to the south on the River Aube, bordering the northernmost vineyards of Burgundy. Currently 75,800 acres (30,685ha) fall within the region allowing for production of about 250 million bottles each year.

The Montagne de Reims

This sloping chalk cliff, approximately 12 miles (19km) long, runs from east to west below the city of Reims down to the river plain. On its

introduction

Above: The white Chardonnay grapes (illustrated) and the black Pinot Noir are the finest champagne grapes.

northern slope are many of the most famous communes of black grape growers. Although this is the most northern point of the delimited area, the Pinot Noir grapes ripen well and provide a vital backbone for the final wines. Split between the Montagne proper and the vineyards closer to Châlons lie some of the most famous of Champagne villages, such as Sillery and Bouzy.

The Vallée de la Marne
The plain of the River Marne, to the west of Reims and Épernay and facing south and southeast, is where the serried ranks of vines lie like the sea, gently rolling in their tidy lines down to the river banks. Here a balance of Pinot Noir, Meunier red, and Chardonnay white grapes are grown, and although there are fewer grand cru here, good blending makes the best of the valley's strengths. The vineyard area sweeps from Tours-sur-Marne through Hautvillers; home of the abbey of Dom Perignon, to below Chateau Thierry with some small pockets lying only 35 miles from Paris.

The Côte des Blancs
The east-facing slopes of the Côte des Blancs are home to the Chardonnay grape, and some of the finest vineyards at Avize, Cramant, and Le Mesnil. Along the sides of the hills the soil contains both chalk and marl, and the vines give

champagne

wine of great delicacy and bouquet — the source of most Blanc de Blancs. Here the scenery is at its finest, as you look from the wooded hilltops across the valley towards Reims.

The Aube
About 60 miles from the southern tip of the Côte des Blancs lie the Aube vineyards, situated around Bar-sur-Aube and Bar-sur-Seine. Here the soils are of a different chalk type and the climate is slightly harsher, but the wines still have a right to the appellation Champagne. The growers of the Aube are great supporters of the Pinot Noir, and are spearheaded by the powerful Union Auboise co-operative with more than 800 members.

THE VINEYARDS AND THE VINES

The wines of the Champagne region are unique for many reasons, but for vineyard owners and growers, some 15-20,000 of them, there are two sets of regulations that rule champagne manufacture with a rod of iron. The *Appellation d'origine contrôllée* laws govern both production and the complex grading of the vineyards that each year gives the price of the grapes: riots have resulted in the past when changes to either were mooted.

Almost all champagne is blended from wines made from many vineyards, and — as with cognac and port — the major houses have to buy the majority of their grapes from small

Below: In 1949 Champagne produced 28 million bottles from just over 28,000 acres (11,500ha) of countryside. By the 1990s the figures had reached 250 million and about 85,000 acres (35,000ha) respectively.

introduction

Above: Despite two world wars — trenches cut through the area for nearly five years — and the depredations of the phylloxera plague that hit the Champagne region in the 1890s, the white chalky slopes are perfect for production of wine.

farmers, who produce less than 10% of the bottled wine. In order that neither side has the upper hand, the vineyards are graded from *Grand Cru* through *Première*, *Deuxième*, and, finally, *Troisième* categories — in a scale called the *Eschelle des Crus* with prices negotiated from year to year. This grading system is controlled by the C.I.V.C. — the *Comité Interprofessionel du Vin de Champagne* — and takes into account the historical quality of the wines each vineyard can produce, although, obviously, the demand for these on the open market is judged on the current quality.

The *Appellation* allows for four grape species, all *Vitis vinifera* grafted onto American rootstock, but actually only two are planted, and these are the Pinot and Chardonnay. The two red Pinot varieties, the Pinot Noir and Pinot Meunier, give richness, depth and backbone, while the white Chardonnay gives elegance, bouquet and delicacy. The vines may be trained in three ways, each designed to suit the aspect and shelter afforded by each vineyard to the different vine types and to restrict the production of each vine — the harder the vine works and the lower the number of grape bunches, the higher the quality of the resulting wine!

The grape-picking almost always begins in September, when an army of volunteers arrives in the region. In order to send the best quality to the presses, all the grapes are picked within two weeks of the harvest beginning!

champagne

WINE PRODUCTION

Almost all champagne is white wine, made mostly from black grapes, a problem overcome by taking great care not to bruise the grapes from picking to pressing. The grapes are quickly sorted and transferred to the *pressoir* and low presses containing up to 8,800lb (4,000kg) of whole bunches of grapes. The first pressing, the *cuvée*, may produce up to 533 U.S. gallons (2,050 litres) and the second, the *taille*, 130 gallons (500 litres) more. Any further juice is not permitted the appellation. The finest wines from the free run juice and cuvée are used to make quality wines; the taille is often sold to *négociants* for blending with lower graded wines.

After pressing, the juice must go through the process of *debourbage*, or clearing, where any impurities and undesirable substances are allowed to fall to the bottom of the holding vat whilst the fermentation is controled by refrigeration. The alcoholic fermentation normally takes place in stainless steel vats and is encouraged by the addition of selected yeasts and, again, is controled by temperature regulation. Following a fermentation period of approximately three weeks, when all the sugars have been turned into alcohol, the wines are run off their lees and the first stage is complete.

The second stage is all-important. After the wines have rested for a short period, they are tasted by the *chef des caves* and the cuvées are assembled. First, wines from the first pickings are blended with those from later days, then those from riper grapes with those from less-ripe or slightly over-ripe grapes, and finally those from different parts of the vineyard. The master blender now has the tools of his trade at his fingers and he must assemble the final cuvées, from both new wines and a proportion of reserve wines from previous years, to be bottled for the second fermentation.

No amount of bookwork or instant knowledge can make up for the years of experience required for this job: my only experience of *assemblage* was greeted with such great jocularity by the supervising *chef des caves* that we both agreed I should return to drinking rather than making champagne. For most blenders the process is one of elimination, and when, finally, the blends are prepared to the satisfaction of the company, the wines are vatted,

introduction

Above: The mechanical processes which dominate modern wine making are becoming more prevalent in champagne production.

fined, and a *liqueur de tirage* is added. This is a careful preparation of older wines, sugar, and cultivated yeasts; it provokes the second fermentation and produces the exact balance of alcohol and degree of effervescence required.

The wines then proceed through the bottling halls, where the bottles are automatically filled to the correct volume and a crown cap or strong staple and intermediate cork is used to close the bottle. As the second fermentation takes place, the used yeast forms a deposit in the bottle and the wines grow in depth and complexity. New regulations state that non-vintage wines must age for 15 months on their lees; vintage wines must age for three years to guarantee the quality expected. One of the most impressive sights in the champagne cellars is the serried ranks of bottles — sometimes up to 250,000 of them — lying both on their sides, *sur lattes*, during the second fermenta-

Below: Following dégorgement, and the ejection of the lees, the champagne is topped up with liqueur d'expédition, a mixture of wine and cane sugar, and then corked.

champagne

tion and ageing, and following *remuage*, neck downwards or *sur pointes*.

The riddling and disgorging of the bottles are part of the grand myth of champagne, but unfortunately a part with which modern technology is rapidly catching up. *Remuage*, or the moving of the sediment from the side of the bottle to the base of the cork, used to be done by highly trained riddlers who could twist, oscillate and tilt up to 50,000 bottles a day in old-fashioned *pupîtres*. Nowadays, modern yeast cultures give rise to a sediment that rolls and coagulates with other solid mass as it descends the bottle and the riddling process is mainly done in large computer-controlled *gyropallettes* which mimic the actions of the *remueur*.

Dégorgement, or the extraction of the sediment, was again done by hand with each bottle quickly opened and then recorked once the cork and sediment had shot out. Now, *dégorgement à la glace* is the method used: conveyor belts carry the wines, neck down, through a freezing trough after which the corks or caps are automatically removed, the sediment ejected and a liqueur added to the bottle. The liqueur replaces the lost liquid and contains a dosage of sugar, which allows the company to determine the style of the final champagne.

TYPES OF WINE

The eventual style of the wine depends not only on the liqueur added after disgorging but also on how the wine was made. Some companies, such as Bollinger and Krug, still ferment their wines in oak casks; some have dabbled with brand new oak or encouraged malolactic fermentation to reduce the biting acidity of the new wines, while others use a greater proportion of the second pressings to add richness and weight. The list below encompasses most offerings to be found commercially:

Dry to sweet gradings
Brut sauvage/extra/zero Bone dry, with little or no sugar in the liqueur (eg Piper)
Brut Dry, with only 0.5-1.5% of sugar added
Extra Dry Off-dry, with 1.5-2.5% added
Sec Medium-dry with 2-4% added
Demi-Sec Medium-sweet with 3-5% sugar
Doux Sweet, desert style with more than 6% of sugar added (eg Mumm)

introduction

Above: Remuage is more often done mechanically in gyropalattes of 500 bottles than by hand on pupîtres of 60 bottles — the traditional way.

House categories
Non-vintage The house style that is reproduced each year by careful buying and blending of reserve wines.
Vintage The finest wines from a particular harvest, aged for twice as long and often with the potential to age in bottle once purchased.
Deluxe or Prestige cuvée The very best the house has to offer, not always a vintage wine but always the best offering from the *chef des caves*.
Rosé Can be any one of the above in quality, and is normally made by blending in some red wines, although some are still made by leaving the pressed wines in contact with the Pinot grape skins for longer.
Blanc de Blancs A wine made only from Chardonnay, and normally exhibiting great finesse and style, if slightly less weight and structure.
Blanc de Noirs A wine made only from Pinot grapes; it can have good depth and a particularly rich and fruity body.
Crémant A wine made with half the pressure, so half as fizzy, produced by adding less sugar and yeast for the second fermentation. Besserat de Bellefon has always produced a good example of this style of champagne.
RD Récent Dégorgement — recently disgorged or taken off the lees. This method is used when the wines are destined for a long life, thus adding a degree of complexity and depth to the champagne. Prime examples have been made by Bollinger and Deutz.

champagne

BUYING, STORING, AND SERVING SPARKLING WINES

Although everyone enjoys the pop of a champagne cork as a bottle is opened, and can admire the towers of foaming glasses that are sometimes built, or even the *sabrage* — opening the bottle with a cavalry sabre — as greatly used in the marketing of Canard-Duchêne, the ideal is somewhat subdued in comparison.

It is true to say that with sparkling wines, as with many other products, the more you pay the more you get in return. The finest wines have the smallest bubbles, the flavor gained from correct ageing on the lees and a reasonable ageing period following the addition of the dosage and the final dressing of the bottle.

Sparkling wines from outside the Champagne region rarely reach the prices of Krug's Clos de Mesnil or Philipponat's Clos des Goisses, but this is often due to the individual attention given to the very small quantities produced and the historical value placed on the very finest vineyard sites. My recommendation is that you should buy what you can afford but always buy better for special occasions, especially in fine restaurants and hotels.

Most champagnes will improve with a little ageing, unless they are specifically made to be drunk very young — representing the first fresh flush of youth — as an aperitif. They should be laid down like any other wine at a stable temperature of ideally about 50°F (10°C). Bottles should be stored either standing up or lying down, in darkened conditions away from the central heating!

Sparkling wines should always be served chilled, ideally between 40-45°F (5-7°C), as this allows the mousse to be released steadily. However, some wines are improved by being slightly colder than others. Again, if drinking very fine wines with food, the wine will be appreciably better for being slightly less chilled, especially if one is to take advantage of the extra nuances gained through the ageing process.

As far as glasses are concerned: the best are tall flutes, because they release the bubbles and aroma steadily sip by sip; flat 'champagne' saucers should be avoided.

introduction

THE BOTTLE

The romantically named larger format bottle sizes have contributed to champagne's fame, but only the standard, half, and magnum are produced in their second fermentation bottle. All other sizes are transferred from the standard size to that ordered.

Quarter Bottle	18.7cl
Half Bottle	37.5cl
Bottle	75cl
Magnum	1.5 litres or 2 bottles
Jeroboam	3 litres or 4 bottles
Rehoboam	4.5 litres or 6 bottles
Methuselah	6 litres or 8 bottles
Salmanazar	9 litres or 12 bottles
Balthazar	12 litres or 16 bottles
Nebuchadnezzar	15 litres or 20 bottles

Below: The normal bottle of champagne contains 75cl of wine.

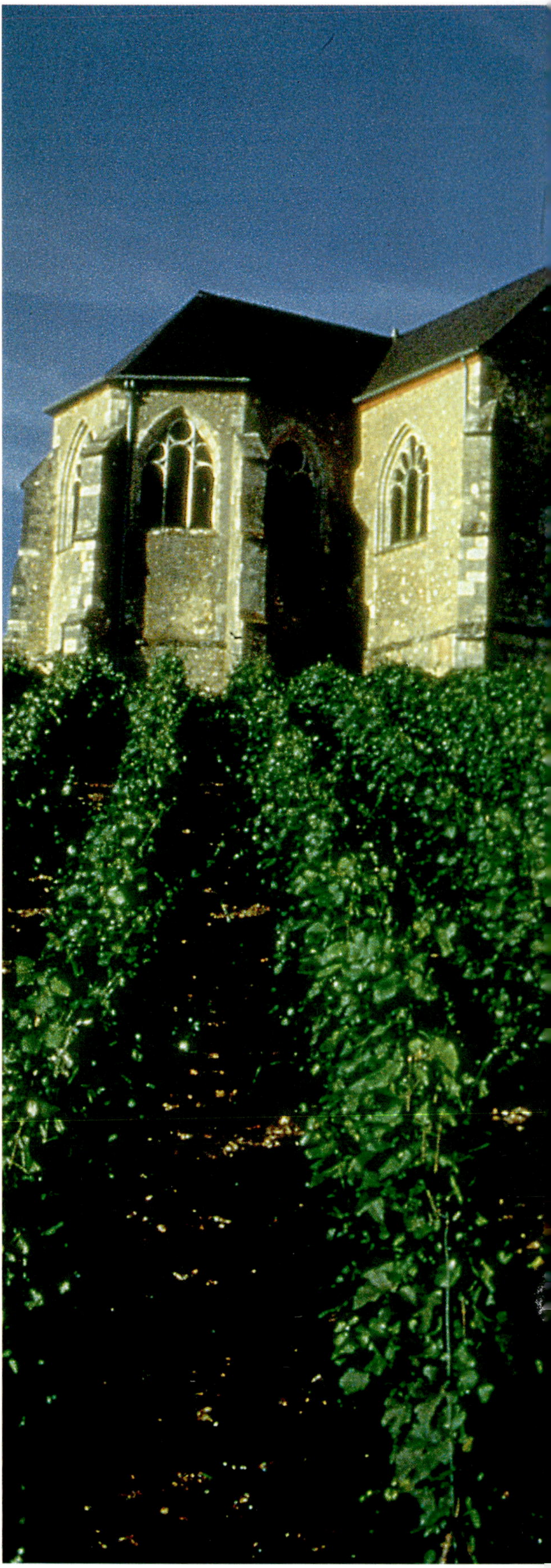

The Wines

champagne

Beaumet

Owners: Gie de Distribution Chateau Malakoff
Established: 1878
Located: Épernay, France
Vineyards: 198 acres (80ha), within the group
Sales: Two million bottles
Exports: 60%
Other Brands: Jeanmarie, Oudinot, Chaurey & Freminet
Deluxe Cuvées: Cuvée Malakoff and Réserve Elysée

A well-established company with good sales on both sides of the Atlantic, Beaumet, owned by Jacques Trouillard since 1977, has considerable grand cru vineyard holdings in the Côte des Blancs, at Avise Cramant, and Chouilly, and these are used to considerable effect in some of the wines.

The sister brands within the group are also considerable sellers. Oudinot has been owned by the Trouillards since 1981 and is made with Jeanmaire in the efficient and modern group winery at Épernay. All of the wines are well made, if a little light in some years, with the Oudinot showing slightly more style, particularly in the Blanc de Noirs. The firm sells the same cuvées under all three labels, with each marque aimed at a different sector of the market.

The Trouillard wines show good ageing and a spicy, soft, style from the mix of Chardonnay and Pinot Meunier used in the blending. A great many wines are offered, from the non-vintage Brut and Rosé, through Blanc de Blancs, Blanc de Noirs, and Brut vintages to the deluxe Malakoff Blanc de Blancs cuvée which is aged for a minimum of seven years and has that distinct, well-matured, Chardonnay style with a rich, long, fruity flavor. Very mature vintages are also offered under the Réserve Elysée label, some up to 30 years old.

the wines

champagne

Billecart-Salmon

Owners: Billecart-Salmon S.A.
Established: 1818
Located: Mareuil-sur-Ay, France
Vineyards: 25 acres (10ha)
Sales: 700,000 bottles
Exports: 60%
Deluxe Cuvées: Nicholas-François Billecart Blanc and Elizabeth Salmon Rosé

Founded by Nicholas-François Billecart only in the early 1800s, although his family had lived in the area since the 16th century, the company was quickly off the mark in some of the emerging markets but then just as quickly struck disaster. In 1830 the company's U.S. agent lost more than 100,000 gold francs and the firm gave up all ideas of exporting, becoming practically dormant.

It was in 1926 that the company, having sold its vineyards, began to expand again, and since that date Billecart has stuck to producing quality rather than quantity. Its champagnes have an edge of delicacy running through the whole range and due, they say, to special fermentation and chilling during the racking process. The company has also installed gyropallettes to ensure an even remuage process.

The company produces a stylish Brut NV, an excellent Brut Rosé N.V., and a selection of vintage wines including the Grand Cuvée, a blend of 80% Chardonnay and 20% Pinot Noir on a Blanc de Blancs. The Brut Cuvée Nicholas Billecart and a Cuvée Elizabeth are both made from almost equal parts Chardonnay and Pinot Noir.

Unusually for a champagne house, almost 20% of Billecart's wines are sold as rosé, a clear indication of the quality and care with which these wines are made.

the wines

champagne

Boizel

Owners: Boizel Chanoine Champagne
Established: 1834
Located: Épernay, France
Vineyards: None directly
Sales: 2.5 million bottles
Exports: 60%
Other Brands: associated with Champagne Chanoine, Abel Lepitre and Philipponnat
Deluxe blend: Joyeau de France

Boizel has been managed since 1984 by one of the most successful ladies in the champagne world, Evelyn Roques-Boizel, the fourth generation of the family. Following financial fluctuations in the early 1990s, a large investment in the company was made by the Paillard-Baijot partnership, and a few years later this was cemented in a partnership between all three families.

Boizel has a modern cuverie in Epernay, and although the house owns no vineyards directly, it buys from a large range of growers — in more than 50 villages — to provide good quality grapes, especially Chardonnay for the immaculate Brut Chardonnay NV, a testament to value for money.

Although not always of the highest quality, Boizel champagnes have recently returned to their best and are well rounded with good flavor and vigor. Non-vintage Brut Réserve and Rosé are produced from predominantly Pinot-based blends, alongside two premium cuvées, the Grand Vintage and the Joyeau de France, which are both more than 60% Pinot Noir.

the wines

champagne

Bollinger

Owners: Bollinger S.A.
Established: 1829
Located: Ay, France
Vineyards: 356 acres (144ha)
Sales: 1.2 million bottles
Exports: 75% or more
Deluxe Cuvées: R.D. and Vieilles Vignes

Possibly the most famous of the great grande marques of champagne, respected for the outstanding quality of the wine, Bollinger was founded in 1829 by a German, Joseph Bollinger, and a Frenchman, Paul Renaudin. Although Bollinger was soon managing the company on his own, the style of wine he first produced has been maintained through years since.

Bollinger has always been based on the family's vineyard holdings in top class sites around the village of Ay; these supply more than 70% of the company's requirements and the continuity of supply has allowed the very full, dry, style of the wine to be maintained. Madame Lily Bollinger was famous for not only continuing production through World War II, touring her vineyards on a bicycle, but for building the company to what it is today. Her nephew, Christian Bizot, is now head of the house and he places even more emphasis on quality than ever before.

The Bollinger Special Cuvée N.V. is full, soft, and rounded with good weight and balance: half the wine is fermented in cask. The Vintage Grande Année and Rosé have that added length and weight from being fermented in oak cask and left to mature for much longer on the lees, and the Deluxe cuvée RD is similar in style if more mature. The Vieilles Vignes are sensational Blanc de Noirs wines with great complexity and add a different dimension to the Bollinger house styles.

the wines

champagne

F. Bonnet

Owners: Rémy-Cointreau
Established: 1920s (re-established in early 1990s)
Located: 12 Allée des Vignobles, Reims, France
Vineyards: 116 acres (47ha) within the group holdings
Sales: 1.2 million bottles
Exports: 45%
Other Brands: Brossault

Run from the 1920s until 1988 by the family of founder Ferdinand Bonnet, the company is now owned by the Remy-Cointreau group and, until very recently, was produced alongside de Venoge. The wines are now made by Dominique Dufour although Cécile Rivault has blended the new Princesse de France.

Bonnet is very much the lesser brand within the group and prices are positioned accordingly, making the wines reasonably good value, although this can vary from label to label. The company produces several styles for the large buyers' own-brand business and also sells a small range of non-vintage cuvées. The newly launched Princesse de France is a soft, delicately styled, wine, which has been marketed deliberately at the young female consumer with good Pinot-based fruit and 20% Chardonnay to add delicacy.

the wines

champagne

Canard-Duchêne

Owners: L.V.M.H.
Established: 1868
Located: Rue de Temple, Reims, France
Vineyards: 45 acres (18ha)
Sales: Three million bottles
Exports: 20%
Deluxe Cuvées: Cuvée Charles VII

Canard-Duchêne has been part of Veuve-Clicquot and a stablemate of the Henriot brand since 1978, and is now indirectly controlled by the massive conglomerate L.V.M.H. It also has the dubious privilege of being the owner of one of the ugliest premises in the region.

One of the problems of belonging to such a big group is that one company always seems to be led to quantity rather than quality. This fate seems to have befallen Canard, currently selling more than three million bottles, and the straightforward Brut NV has been less than convincing recently. The two prestige cuvées, the vintage Brut Patrimoine and the deluxe Cuvée Charles VII, can be better performers but again are disappointing on recent tastings.

The most that can be said for these wines is that they can offer reasonable value and that, although not impressive, the winemaking is rarely at fault, so simple fruit and little complexity is the reward here.

the wines

champagne

de Castellane

Owners: Groupe Laurent-Perrier
Established: 1895
Located: Rue du Verdun, Épernay, France
Vineyards: 247 acres (100ha) within group
Sales: 2.5 million bottles
Exports: 25%
Other Brands: Maxim's de Paris and many others

An old-fashioned house that has only recently begun to modernize production and the style of its wines, De Castellane was founded by an aristocratic Provençale, whose ideas on traditional fermentation in oak casks were practiced by the company until the late 1980s. The Laurent-Perrier Company has taken a controlling share in de Castellane and the wines have become slightly lighter and more delicate since. It is possibly the easiest house to find from the outskirts of Épernay due to the famous domed tower that rises high above the other buildings.

The wines bearing the Croix Rouge de Saint André on the label are predominantly Pinot Noir and Pinot Meunier, and are relatively mature with a rounded style, whether vintage or non-vintage. The Cuvée Royale and vintage Cuvée Florens de Castellane are made from Chardonnay, and the Cuvée Commodore at least 80% Pinot Noir. The best of these in flavor and value is the Royale Chardonnay, which is made from highly rated vineyards and shows a delicacy and finesse that sometimes escapes the other wines. The Vicomte de Castellane selection harkens back to the history of the company: 15-20% of the wine has remained in cask for at least a year.

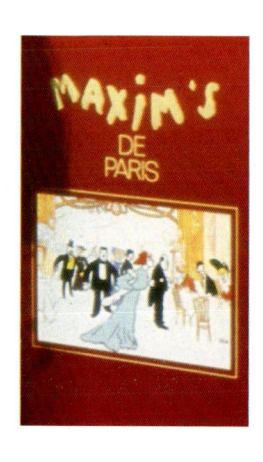

the wines

champagne

Charles de Cazanove

Owners: Lombard Family and SAME Group
Established: 1811
Located: Rue des Cotelles, Epernay, France
Vineyards: 50 acres (20ha) through a sister company
Sales: Three million bottles
Exports: 20%
Other Brands: Lanvin, Magenta
Deluxe Cuvées: Stradivarius

Founded by Charles-Gabriel de Cazanove in Avize, at the heart of the Côte des Blancs, de Cazanove is today based in Épernay. The company was family-run for almost a century and a half until 1958, when it was sold to the Martini Company, which in turn passed ownership on to Moët-Hennessy in 1979. The company is now owned by the Lombard family, who has proceeded to invest heavily in bringing the firm's premises and equipment up to date.

This impressive investment has paid dividends in the wines. The non-vintage Brut Classique, made predominantly from Pinot Noir, is a full-bodied fruity champagne with plenty of class. The Rosé Brut is similar in style, with approximately 95% Chardonnay in its blend. De Cazanove also produces a Chardonnay-based non-vintage called Brut Azur — quite a full-bodied wine, which is worth looking out for. There are three vintage cuvées, the Brut, Brut Azur Premier Cru, and the Tête de Cuvée Stradivarius, again based respectively on Pinot Noir for the former and Chardonnay for the latter two.

the wines

champagne

Guy Charbaut

Owners: Guy Charbaut
Established: 1948
Located: Mareuil-sur-Ay, France
Vineyards: 123.5 acres (50ha)
Sales: 100,000 bottles
Exports: 50%

This was a family company that was founded in 1948, by André Charbaut as a grower producing champagne only from the family vineyards, but over the last 50 years grew to the point where sales had reached almost a million bottles and the company had scored a hit by supplying their champagne to the American airlines TWA and Pan-Am. In order to supplement the vineyard produce grapes were bought in from a mixture of grand and premier cru sites which were classified at between 90 and 100%. In 1995 the negociant side of the company was sold to the Vranken Group, and René and Guy Charbaut returned to the roll of grower producer.

This great increase lead to a slight fall in the overall quality of the wines and the current aim is to revive the style and quality that was once shown by the Certificate wines. The new Brut and Cuvée de Réserve are both one-third Chardonnay and two-thirds Pinot Noir and the vintage Brut is made to the same recipe. The Rosé Brut is made by the saignée method where the free run juice from red grapes is allowed to gain color during pressing and has traditionally been the finest wine that the family has produced, the current cuvée is 10% Chardonnay and 90% Pinot Noir and should age quite well.

From zero to 100,000 bottles is a large step in the right direction, and with 123.5 acres (50ha) of excellent vineyards there is more to come from this illustrious family company.

the wines

champagne

Veuve Clicquot-Ponsardin

Owners: Veuve Clicquot-Ponsardin
Established: 1772
Located: Reims, France
Vineyards: 700 acres (285ha)
Sales: 10 million bottles
Exports: 50%
Deluxe Cuvées: La Grande Dame

One of the oldest of the great champagne houses, Veuve Clicquot owes its great name and style to the widow of the founder, Nicole Barbe-Clicquot, who ran the company for 60 years after the death of her husband. During this period she developed the process of production with the help of her chief wine-maker, Antoine Muller, and perfected the method of clearing the wine, known as *remuage*.

Her partner in later years, Edouard Werlé, established many export markets and it was his descendant, the Comte Bertrand de Mun, who brought Clicquot into this century and refined the massive vineyard estate. This now covers a substantial area, spread throughout the districts of the region, and includes many of the grand cru in the Côte des Blancs, such as Avize and Le Mesnil, and in the Montagne de Reims, such as Bouzy.

The cellars at Clicquot are a perfect example of modern winemaking and investment in technology. All the wines are fermented in stainless steel and the process of ageing, blending, riddling, and disgorging is fully controlled. In full flow, the disgorging hall is something to be seen, if a bit hard on the ears!

The wines have always shown a predominance of Pinot, and the Yellow Label Brut is full-bodied and deep tasting with good age. The Réserve Brut and Rosé are both vintage-dated and show great elegance and depth. The La Grande Dame deluxe Cuvée is also vintage-dated and is a very big wine with lots of mature depth and finesse, one of the finest champagnes one can lay down for further ageing.

the wines

champagne

Cordornìu

Owners: Cordornìu Group
Established: Original family holdings are four centuries old
Located: San Sadurni díAnoia, Penedés
Sales: 10 million cases, within the group
Other Brands: Raimat
Deluxe Cuvées: Anna de Codornìu Chardonnay Brut

The other of the two giants of the Spanish sparkling wine trade. Codornìu was founded by Don Josep Raventòs, one of the first producers of sparkling wines by the traditional method in Spain; his forefathers had been winemakers since the 16th century.

Today the largest producer in Spain, this is solely due to sales of its house brand and the subsidiary Raimat, which was one of the first to introduce an estate-bottled Chardonnay wine, rather than ownership of other houses. The use of Chardonnay has been continued through the main cuveés and some Pinot Noir as also been recently introduced. Under wine maker Miguel Gurpide, Codornìu has become the foremost innovator in quality Cava and the house's recent wines lead the way in competing in the international quality markets. Codornìu has vast cellars — almost 12 miles (19km) — and buy in grapes from several hundred growers.

The 1551 Brut is based on the traditional assemblage of Macabeo and Xarel-lo but with the Parellada replaced by 20% Chardonnay. The Raventòs Brut has up to 50% Chardonnay and the deluxe Anna has 85%. The wines bottled under the Raimat label are the best and represent real value, the Gran Brut has good oak tones and well developed rich fruit leading to a well balanced finish with plenty of finesse.

the wines

champagne

Deutz

Owners: C.D.G.V. (61% owned by Louis Roederer)
Established: 1838
Located: 16 Rue Jeanson, Ay, France
Vineyards: 104 acres (42ha)
Sales: One million bottles
Exports: 35%
Deluxe Cuvées: William Deutz

Another company founded in the 1830s, a golden era for the Champenoises. Deutz was founded, like many other houses, by a German wine-maker, in this case William Deutz, who had previously been engaged by Bollinger. He was joined by Pierre Gelderman, whose wealth enabled the company to grow substantially over the next 50 years.

The firm suffered a great setback in the riots of 1911 and lost some sales momentum when the ageing cellars were badly damaged. During the 1980s Deutz was one of the first champagne companies to expand into the "New World" wine countries and operations were set up in both California and New Zealand. During this period, the company also released selections of late disgorged wines, which showed very well the advantages in depth and richness, that extra ageing on the lees could provide.

By 1993 the company was in need of further capitalization and Louis Roederer bought a controlling interest. The wines tend to be slightly dumb to start with, but can develop over time, with the vintage Blanc de Blancs showing great subtlety and delicacy. Alongside the vintage Brut and Rosé cuvées the company also produces a kosher non-vintage wine and deluxe brut and rosé wines called Cuvée William Deutz. The vintage rosé wines are particularly powerful and are normally made from 100% Pinot Noir.

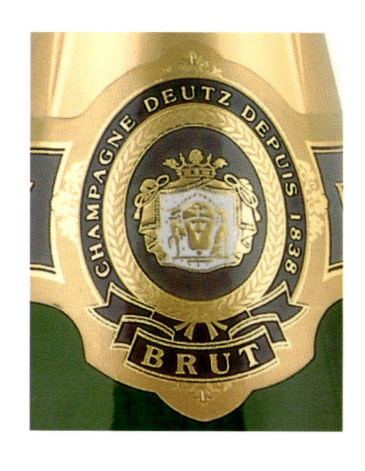

the wines

champagne

Devaux

Owners: Veuve A. Devaux
Established: 1846
Located: Bar-sur-Seine, France
Vineyards: 2,470 acres (1,000ha)
Sales: 2.5 million bottles
Exports: 30%
Other Brands: Léonce d'Albe and Nicole d'Aurigny
Deluxe Cuvées: Millésime Brut

A great example of what can be produced by the co-operative wine-makers in France, the Veuve Devaux brand belongs to the Union Auboise, a grouping of more than 800 growers who between them have more than 2,000 acres of vines.

Made up from 12 co-operatives with vineyards situated in the outlying Aube region, under the control of wine-maker Claude Thibaut, the group unsurprisingly makes its champagnes from a very large proportion of Pinot Noir, about 10-12% Chardonnay, and very little Pinot Meunier. Although the co-operatives supply a great deal of grapes and wine to the major volume producers and many grand marques, these wines are very good indeed.

Many non-vintage wines are produced; the Grand Réserve and Blanc de Noirs Brut, and the Cuvée Rosé and Oeil de Perdrix Rosé, are benchmark wines with attractively fruity flavors. The vintage selections receive a minimum of three years ageing in bottle, which allows the wines to grow in style and offer a fuller biscuity flavor, while still remaining perfectly in balance. It should not be remarkable given the vineyard holdings of this grouping if the wines continue to improve and the current excellent reputation is further enhanced.

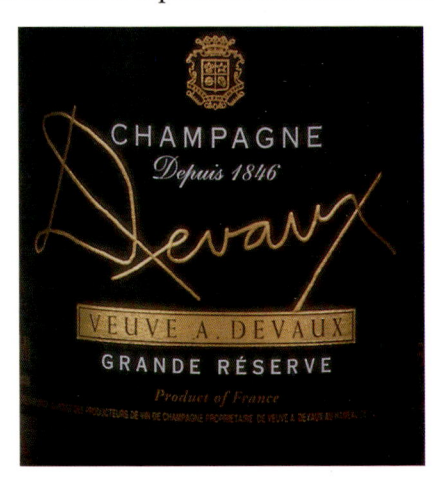

the wines

champagne

Domain Chandon

Owners: Moët & Chandon
Established: 1973
Located: Yountville, California
Vineyards: 740 acres (300ha) or more
Sales: Five million bottles
Exports: Less than 20%
Other Brands: Etoile and Shadow Creek for all export markets

The frontrunner of the invasion from Champagne, Moët & Chandon, and parent company L.V.M.H., have established sparkling wine ventures around the world, in Australia through Domaine Chandon and the Green Point label, in New Zealand through the Veuve Clicquot interests in Pelorus from Cloudy Bay, and in Spain through Cava Chandon and the Torre del Gall label.

Grapes for the Californian venture are sourced from Carneros and Mount Veeder, and the range of wines produced is identical under both labels. The plantings are of the three traditional champagne grapes plus a little Pinot Blanc. The policy in California is for all the wines to be non-vintage, although this does discount the marketing options available for the better cuvées.

The Blanc de Noirs is a blend of 81% Pinot Noir and 19% Pinot Meunier, all sourced from Carneros, reserve wines from back to 1993 and was aged for 30 months on its lees. It has a very pale salmon-pink tinge to its color and a full soft flavor with a light clean finish. The Etoile wines have a marked Chardonnay influence and the standard Chandon Reserve Brut is a blend of all four grape types.

the wines

champagne

Duval-Leroy

Owners: The Duval Family
Established: 1859
Located: 69 Avenue de Bammental, Vertus, France
Vineyards: 346 acres (140ha)
Exports: 37%
Sales: 6.5 million bottles
Other Brands: E. Michel, Paul Vertay

The Duval-Leroy Company has grown significantly in the recent past and is now one of the major players in terms of both volume and quality sales. The company was established in 1859 but is currently run by Carol Duval, who, with her wine-maker Hervé Jestin, has elevated the quality at this family company beyond all expectations. Quality marketing is now the watchword with Duval, and separate companies are being set up in each individual major market.

The company's Fleur de Champagne Brut N.V. is made each year from 65-85% Chardonnay (depending on the harvest), and has considerable elegance and finesse. Non-vintage Fleur de Champagne Blanc de Blancs and Blanc de Noirs are also made; these show great consistency and good fruit flavors. Those who live in the UK have been exceptionally lucky to be able to follow these wines' continued association with the supermarket group J. Sainsbury.

Finer still are the Brut vintages and the older vintages of Cuvée de Roys, which was 95% Chardonnay. There should be a new cuvée to celebrate the millennium and it will be well worth looking out for.

the wines

champagne

Nicolas Feuillatte

Owners: Centre Vinicole de la Champagne Co-operative
Established: 1976
Located: BP 210 Chouilly, France
Vineyards: 4,700 acres (1,900ha)
Sales: 2.9 million bottles
Exports: 30%
Other Brands: St Nicholas, St. Maurice, De Prayeres, and others
Deluxe Cuvées: Palmes d'Or

One of the most recent and most successful partnerships in champagne is that between Nicolas Feuillatte and the C.V.C. at Chouilly, in the Côte des Blancs. In the early 1970s Feuillatte was fortunate enough to inherit a small vineyard in the Champagne region and a few years later he took his marketing expertise, gained in New York, to the C.V.C. co-operative whose 4,800 members farm more than 4,000 acres in some of the finest areas of Champagne.

With such a depth of raw material to draw on, the wines can show extremely well, and the non-vintage Brut Cuvée Speciale is a delightfully easy-drinking glass with good clean fruit. Non-vintage Blanc de Blancs and rosé wines are also made, as well as a standard Brut Réserve Particulière, which can be a bit variable.

Of the vintage and deluxe cuvées, the Cuvée Speciale Palmes d'Or (a blend of 40% Pinot Noir, 40% Chardonnay, and 20% Pinot Meunier) has a rich mature flavor and stylish finish. The two Brut Premier wines are heavily Pinot-based and on occasion have been a little too assertive. Again, the co-operative movement is seen to make good wines here, only lacking sometimes in a little elegance.

the wines

champagne

Freixenet

Owners: Freixenet Group
Established: 1889
Located: San Sadurni díAnoia, Penedes
Sales: Seven million cases, within the group
Other Brands: Castellblanch, Segura Viudas, Conde de Caralt, Canals Nubiola
Deluxe Cuvées: Cuvée DS

One of the two giants of the Spanish sparkling wine trade, the company was founded by Don Pedro Ferrer and established as an industry leader following his marriage to Don Delores Sala who also came from a traditional winemaker's family.

Although always one of the major forces in the production of sparkling wine, Freixenet's growth in pursuit of Cordonìu, its major rival, has been very visible over the last 20 years with, amongst others, the takeover of the old Rumasa producers within the Cava industry as well as investment in may of the new world wine regions. The enormous growth of these two rivals has brought Cava production to the fore in terms of volume production and Freixenet remain firmly imbedded at the traditional heart in Spain, firmly against the introduction of non-native grape varieties and blends.

Most famous for its Cordon Negro Brut in the black bottle, the various wines of Freixenet are based round a blend of the traditional grapes of the Penedés — MacabÈo, Parellada, and Xarel-lo — and the different cuvées tend to differ through the proportion of the latter two varieties. The best wines are the vintage Brut nature, with its slightly lower dosage, and the Rosado Brut made from the black grapes, Garnacha and Monastrell.

the wines

champagne

Gosset

Owners: Cointreau Family
Established: 1584
Located: Rue Jules Blondeau, Ay, France
Vineyards: None
Sales: 600,000 bottles
Exports: 40%
Other Brands: Ivernel

As the label states, Gosset is, "*La plus ancienne Maison de Vins de la Champagne*" — the oldest champagne manufacturer. Founded as a wine producer in 1584 by Pierre Gosset, the family had four centuries of unbroken ownership until 1994, when the company was bought by Max Cointreau. Elected to stand with its peers in 1992 as an official grande marque house, Gosset has always produced big, deep-flavored, wines with an ability to stand cellaring.

Fortunately, the new owners are well-versed in the traditions of quality and, under Béatrice Cointreau and the wine-maker Jean-Pierre Mareignier, the wines have continued to show very well. The wines are all well-aged, some in wood, and avoid malolactic fermentation so ensuring a long life. The Brut Excellence is somewhat straightforward, and is almost equal parts Chardonnay and Pinot. The real stars are the older Grande Réserve Brut and the Grand Millésime Brut, which are big wines with a toasted biscuit richness of body and immeasurable length, the vintage wine not always out-tasting its non-vintage sibling.

These are not inexpensive wines, but they are rich enough to match many foods and are a must for the cellar of the champagne collector.

the wines

champagne

Heidsieck & Co. Monopole

Owners: Vranken Group
Established: 1834
Located: Avenue de Champagne, Epernay, France
Vineyards: 320 acres (130ha) within group
Sales: 1.2 million bottles
Exports: 75%
Deluxe Cuvées: Daimant Blue Vintage

A company with a rather chequered history, Heidsieck & Co. has had many owners since being founded in 1834 by Henri-Louis Walbaum. Between 1972 and 1996 the firm received a massive marketing boost when it was owned by Seagram and run in conjunction with G.H. Mumm, but the company has since been bought by the ambitious Vranken group to spearhead its branded image in the world export markets. Unfortunately, the purchase did not include the finest vineyards the company had owned, but did bring another 320 acres (130ha) into the Vranken fold.

The wines, always better known as Monopole, are unashamedly Pinot-based with traditionally 60 to 70% of Pinot Noir and Meunier. This gives a rich soft and fruity wine with good structure and definition. The current blends are well supported by the parent group's access to a huge supply of grapes from different areas, including many top-rated vineyards, and it will be interesting to see how the style develops when the wines that came with the purchase are exhausted.

The marketing thrust of the company lies behind the non-vintage Blue Top Monopole and the premium cuvée Daimant Blue, which have been subtly repackaged with more defined labeling to reinforce the heritage of the house. Vintage blanc and rosé wines are also sold under the Dry Monopole label.

the wines

champagne

Charles Heidsieck

Owners: Rémy-Cointreau
Established: 1851
Located: Boulevard Henry Vasnier, Reims, France
Vineyards: 16 acres (47ha) with other group members
Sales: Two million bottles
Exports: 25%
Deluxe Cuvées: Champagne Charlie

Famous throughout the world, Charles Heidsieck is one of the great champagnes, founded in 1851 by the original Champagne Charlie, Charles-Camille Heidsieck, and his brother-in-law Ernest Henriot.

Charles Heidsieck's fame was built on 10 years of amazing sales in the USA: from 1851 to 1861 sales grow from nothing to 300,000 bottles. However, this almost came to nothing, when Charles Heidsieck, who was on one of his sales trips to the USA, was arrested by the Unionists for dealing with the Confederate Army. He returned to France a shadow of his former self but fortunately his sons and grandsons took over and developed new markets that gave the company more security.

Control of the company stayed with the Heidsieck family until 1976, when Joseph Henriot, a descendent of the original partner, Ernest, took over. The company was, in turn, sold to Rémy-Martin in 1985 who instigated a huge turn around in the winemaking and quality of the wines. Under Rémy's control, a small vineyard holding has been bought, better grapes bought in, and Daniel Thibault installed as the chef des caves.

The non-vintage Brut Réserve, now one of the very best on the market with its full biscuity aroma and deep rich flavor, is made from only the first pressings of grapes from a complex blend of different vineyards, with a judicious proportion of reserve wines from earlier years. Heidsieck has even gone so far as to put the "laying down" dates on the back label to show how long the wines have aged in cellar. Alongside the vintage blanc and rosé, two prestige cuvées are produced, of which the older vintages of Champagne Charlie really stand out.

the wines

champagne

Jacquart

Owners: The Co-opérative Régionale des Vins de Champagne
Established: 1962
Located: Rue Gosset, Reims, France
Vineyards: 2,470 acres (1,000ha)
Sales: 4.9 million bottles
Exports: 20%
Other Brands: Ritz

Another strong showing from the co-operative movement in the Champagne region. Jacquart was launched as the premier brand of the co-operative in the 1970s, and in order to give its full backing to the brand, a company was formed to give marketing backing with each member as a shareholder.

Although half the wines are sold as own label champagnes, a great deal of time and effort has been sunk into the brand and today it is one of the major players in the volume market. Under winemaker Richard Dailly the wines have shown a consistency of quality; they are based on an almost equal partnership between Chardonnay, Pinot Noir, and Pinot Meunier in the non-vintage wines, and Chardonnay and Pinot Noir in the vintage selections.

The main thrust lies behind those labeled under the Cuvée Mosaïque label, but the Cuvée Nominée wines, especially the Rosé are as good, if not better, in most years.

the wines

champagne

Krug

Owners: Rémy-Cointreau
Established: 1842
Located: Rue Coquebert, Reims, France
Vineyards: 52 acres (21ha)
Sales: 450-500,000 bottles
Exports: 83%

The house of Krug was founded in 1842, when Joseph Krug, who had earlier left the Jacquesson Company, founded his own house in Reims. One version of his leaving had it that he was unhappy of the quality of the champagne that would be associated with his name: if this was true then he and his descendants have made it their aim in life to ensure that no other house can be held in greater regard for quality.

In order to do this, the Krug philosophy has always been to select the finest grapes from the highest classed vineyards, ferment in oak casks, and to blend judiciously from well-aged stock. All three grapes are used to construct the blends and for the Grand Cuvée up to 50% of reserve wines, which may be 15 years old, are used to give depth, finesse, and power. For those of us fortunate enough to have tasted still wines with the Krugs before the second fermentation, it is no wonder that the final product is so good.

Four wines are produced and it could be said that they are all deluxe cuvées, at the very least, they cost as much as any other house's premier offerings. The Grand Cuvée is the pinnacle of achievement; although a non-vintage this is never less than great wine, and has both elegant aroma and great complexity. The Rosé is quite delicious and totally balanced, while the vintages are massive multi-layered wines. The most modern of the Krug offerings is the single vineyard Clos de Mesnil, a 100% Chardonnay, which is made from a vineyard purchased in 1971. The first wines were sold from the 1979 vintage and since then it has produced sublime wines that will take many years to come round.

the wines

champagne

Charles Lafitte

Owners: Vranken-Monopole Group
Established: 1976
Located: Place Tritant, Bouzy, France
Vineyards: 395 acres (160ha)
Sales: 1.5 million bottles
Exports: 38%
Other Brands: Demoiselle, Sacotte, Barancourt, Charbaut & Vranken
Deluxe Cuvée: Orgueil de France

A very large grouping of labels put together by the Belgian Paul-François Vranken, which has grown considerably since being founded in 1976. Total sales of nine million bottles are spread between the above labels and the Heidsieck Monopole brand purchased at the end of 1996.

The company bought the famous house of Barancourt, in 1994, and the best wines here are under their vintage Cuvée des Fondateurs label, which like many of the wines this company has produced need a long time to reach their best. Barancourt also are one of the few producers of Bouzy Rouge, a still red wine under the Coteaux Champenois Appellation. They then added the negociant label of Charbaut in 1995 although not the vineyards and winemaking skills of the Charbaut Family.

The wines produced under the Demoiselle label are based around Chardonnay and show good fruit and fresh flavours, whilst the Charles Lafitte wines are a blend of Pinot Noir, meunier and Chardonnay and have perhaps the greater balance and length. The current 1985 Orgueil de France vintage from Lafitte shows good style for a wine of considerable age.

With such a large volume of wine coming from the Vranken cellars there seems to be a slight similarity in style amongst the many labels and although they offer good value, the finest of flavours are sometimes a little elusive.

the wines

champagne

Lanson

Owners: Marne & Champagne Diffusion
Established: 1760
Located: Boulevard Lundy, Reims, France
Vineyards: None
Sales: 6.2 million bottles
Exports: 60%
Deluxe Cuvées: Noble
Other Brands: Baron Edouard Massé

Although established in 1760 by Francois Delamotte, it was not until his son was joined by Jean-Baptiste Lanson in 1828 that the firm really took off, and 30 years later the company changed its name to Lanson when Jean-Baptiste's two nephews took control.

The company built up a vineyard holding of over 500 acres (202.5ha) during the next century, but in 1970 the Ricard Company bought a 48% shareholding, family control was lost, and a whirlwind of changes took place over the next 20 years. First, in 1980, the owners of Pommery bought the Ricard shareholding, and then took control of the whole company. The next sale was to B.S.N., the giant brewer and foods group, in 1983; B.S.N. then sold the company to L.V.M.H. in 1990. L.V.M.H. kept the vineyards and sold the brands and premises to the huge BOB (buyer's own brand) company Marne & Champagne, which wanted a major name to spearhead its brand challenge.

Such immense changes have undoubtedly taken their toll on the quality of the wines, and it is only recently that the flagship Black Label has returned to something like its previous style. However, the old vintages of Lanson are always worth buying up and the prestige cuvées should be watched carefully as they previously showed extremely well.

the wines

champagne

Laurent-Perrier

Owners: Veuve Laurent-Perrier & Co.
Established: 1812
Located: Avenue de Champagne, Tours-sur-Marne, France
Vineyards: 259 acres (105ha)
Sales: Six million bottles
Exports: 60%
Other Brands: Lemoine

One of the major success stories of postwar champagne production, the Laurent Perrier Company now owns the very respectable houses of de Castellane, Delamotte, and Salon. From lowly coopers at the turn of the 19th century, the company is now one of the largest in the region, and very well respected for the quality control it brings to production.

The big changes have all been achieved since Bernard de Nonancourt took the reins after World War 2 and over the last 50 years his two winemakers have produced wines that are a tribute not only to the grapes but also to the masterful skills of the blender. The non-vintage Brut, Rosé, and Ultra Brut are all good straightforward wines that have class and elegance, and will be all the better for a year or two in your cellar. The vintage wines are better with both the Brut and Grand Siècle showing great style and finesse.

The best wine, however, must be the non-vintage Grand Siècle, a blend of three vintages and one which, since a visit to both houses one weekend, I have always seen as the best to taste alongside the Krug Grand Cuvée, as the finest blended champagnes available. Current blends feature wines from the 1980s with the addition of 1990 to the current cuvée, and these are both Grand Siècle at its very best.

the wines

champagne

Lindauer and Deutz

Owners: Montana
Established: 1952
Located: Marlborough, Auckland, New Zealand
Vineyards: 1,500 acres (600ha)
Sales: Five million bottles
Exports: 50%

From the original first plantings in the 1940s, Montana has grown to be New Zealand's largest producer with up to 3,000 acres (1,200ha) of vineyards in production and under contract. Founded by Ivan Yukich, and now a publicly quoted company, Montana produces a large range of still wines from various regions of New Zealand, two very high quality sparkling wines under the Lindauer label and, in conjunction with Champagne Deutz, under the Deutz Marlborough Cuvée label.

The sparkling wines have benefited greatly from the Seagram shareholding in the parent company and the resulting marketing clout that this brings. The Deutz link has also worked well and was the better of the wines that Deutz produced in New Zealand and in the USA.

The Lindauer wines were first marketed in 1981 and are based around Pinot Noir and Chardonnay with some other grapes involved in constructing the assemblage; a premium cuvée, Lindauer Special Reserve is also made which has up to 70% Pinot Noir.

The Deutz wines, a 50% Pinot Noir and 50% Chardonnay Deutz Brut and a Blanc de Blancs from 100% Chardonnay, are made under the supervision of Andre Lallier from France and the Montana cellarmaster Peter Hubscher. Both labels offer good value and have a youthful fruity style with some finesse when kept for a little longer.

the wines

champagne

Mercier

Owners: L.V.M.H.
Established: 1858
Located: Avenue de Champagne, Epernay, France
Vineyards: 1,900 acres (772ha) with Moët & Chandon
Sales: 6.17 million bottles
Exports: 18%
Deluxe Cuvées: Eugene Mercier

The famous Mercier Company was formed in 1858 when Eugéne Mercier drew together five other companies and named them Mercier — Union de Propriétaires. Eugéne Mercier was the greatest showman in the history of champagne and was renowned for his marketing abilities. His famous cask for the Paris exhibition was built to contain more than 20,000 litres (5,280 U.S. gallons) and he had it delivered to the halls through the streets of Paris by an impressive oxen train. He was also involved in an unplanned stunt when his famous hot-air balloon broke loose and traveled across the border into Germany, complete with a party of the general public who had boarded only to taste the wines.

Since 1970, the brand has been owned by Moët & Chandon who have continued to focus on the French market, where Mercier is the market leader. Although the brand is sometimes seen as a lesser label than Moët, the wines are of consistent quality and good value.

From the non-vintage to the prestige Eugéne Mercier, there is very little Chardonnay used, and many of the wines contain at least 40% Pinot Meunier, which gives a very soft, approachable, style. Mercier is one of the few houses to produce both brut and demi-sec versions of their non-vintage rosé wine.

the wines

champagne

Moët & Chandon

Owners: L.V.M.H.
Established: 1743
Located: Avenue de Champagne, Epernay, France
Vineyards: 1,897 acres (768ha)
Sales: 25 million bottles
Exports: 83%
Deluxe Cuvées: Dom Perignon

The cornerstone of the champagne trade, Moët & Chandon has been at the forefront of vineyard and wine development since the days of founder Claude Moët, and although the vineyard totals rise and fall within the group, more than 2,470 acres (1,000ha) are owned, making the company the biggest grower by far.

In the first half of the 19th century the fame of the house was such that it was already the largest exporter and producer, further expansion was in line by the end of the century, and later in between the two world wars, Moët also launched the first deluxe cuvée — named after the famous monk Dom Perignon.

After floating on the French Bourse, the company expanded further by acquiring Ruinart in 1963, Mercier in 1970, purchased the perfume house of Christian Dior in 1971, merged with the Louis Vuitton-owned Veuve Clicquot and Canard-Duchêne in the 1980s, bought Pommery in 1990 and finally bought and sold Lanson a few years later. All this has left the group selling 55 million bottles, about a fifth of all champagne sales!

The Moët wines themselves are classically styled and impressive for their uniform quality. The Brut Imperial or White Star has been joined by a Brut 1er Cru and a Brut Rosé: all are good examples of the biggest knowing quite well how to produce the best. The vintage wines are often superb and the Dom Perignon almost as good as its price should demand!

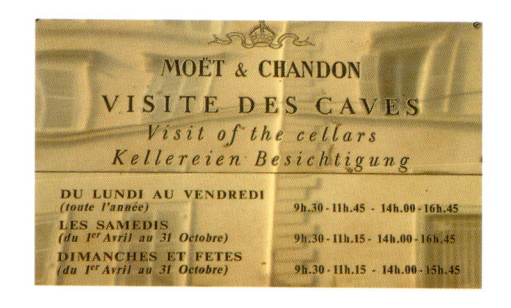

the wines

champagne

G. H. Mumm

Owners: Seagram
Established: 1827
Located: Rue de Champ-de-Mars, Reims, France
Vineyards: 538 acres (218ha)
Sales: Eight million bottles
Exports: 66%
Deluxe Cuvées: René Lalou and Grand Cordon

The firm was founded by two German brothers and run by their son until 1914, when it was confiscated at the outbreak of the war; later, in 1920, was auctioned by the French Government. The company was bought by a group of investors but it was René Lalou, connected to the Dubonnet family, who took control and oversaw the period of growth that carried on right until 1972.

In the meantime, the giant Seagram Group had purchased a large shareholding and, on the acquisition of Chauvet in 1969, took control of the group, which by this time also encompassed Perrier-Jouët. Heidsieck & Co. Monopole was also bought in the 1970s but was later sold to the Vranken group, without its best vineyards.

After a poor period of winemaking, the basic Cordon wines are back on song, under wine-maker Dominique Demarville, and because of the Pinot base are softly fruity and quite instantly attractive. The Cramant Blanc de Blanc has a gently sparkling style and the two prestige cuvées are reliable and good quality, if difficult to see as value for money. Always popular in the United States, Mumm is still one of the largest brands in champagne.

the wines

champagne

Mumm Cuvée Napa

Owners: Seagram
Established: 1987
Located: Napa Valley, California
Vineyards: Sourced from various Napa vineyards
Sales: 2.5 million bottles
Exports: Less than 20%
Deluxe Cuvées: DVX

Established following Seagram's venture into American sparkling wines, which began in the late 1970s, the use of the Mumm marque was squarely aimed at utilising the group's ownership of one of the USA's most popular French Champagne marques — and how well it has succeeded! A joint venture with Twee Jongegezellen also produces Cap Cuvée Mumm in South Africa.

The Mumm operation is extremely modern with up-to-date wine-making equipment and exacting requirements. Every aspect of the process from picking and grape selection is aimed at maximising the condition the grapes arrive in at the press house and ensuring that the most flavor and freshness is available to wine maker Rob McNeill. Again the traditional Pinot Noir and Chardonnay are the mainstay of the blends with a little Pinot Gris in the Blanc de Blancs selection.

A full range of wines is on offer from Mumm, including the Blanc de Blancs, Rose Blanc de Noirs, Brut Prestige and the vintage DVX and Winery Lake wines, which offer both quality and extremely good value for money.

All in all, Mumm have come closest to equalling the output from the Champagne region in France, and deserve the reputation that goes with it.

the wines

champagne

Perrier-Jouët

Owners: Seagram
Established: 1811
Located: Avenue de Champagne, Epernay, France
Vineyards: 185 acres (75ha)
Sales: 2.8 million bottles
Exports: 75%
Deluxe Cuvées: La Belle Époque

Founded by a M. Nicolas-Marie Perrier, who joined his wife's name to his own to form the brand Perrier-Jouët, this company was quickly off the mark in export markets and has never looked back. The son of the founder, Charles Perrier, further expanded exports and the reputation of the wines, particularly with the royal courts around Europe. Ownership has since passed through several members of the founder's extended family until in 1959 Seagram — through its Mumm subsidiary — took a majority shareholding in the company.

Under the control of Seagram, the Budin family have continued to be involved and the current wine-maker Hervé Deschamps has maintained the high reputation of the wines. The basic Grand Brut is light and fruity in style with a large Pinot emphasis, and the Blason de France Brut and Rosé are of better quality and show greater finesse.

The bottles for which the house is most famous are the art nouveau enamelled Belle Époque prestige cuvée. Beautifully dressed bottles with the finest wines based on Grand Cru Chardonnay grapes from Cramant. These have the capability to age for many years and, though light in weight, are extremely rich with great finesse. A special, very limited, cuvée has been launched for the millennium, which includes a stay at the company's Maison Belle Époque, a shrine to art nouveau lovers.

the wines

champagne

Philipponat

Owners: BCC Group
Established: 1910
Located: Mareuil-sur-Ay, France
Vineyards: 40 acres (16.5ha)
Sales: 500,000 bottles
Exports: 60%
Other Brands: Associated with Abel Lepitre, and others within BCC
Deluxe Cuvées: Clos des Goisses

Although associated with producing champagne since the 17th century, it wasn't until 1910 that the Philipponat brothers, Pierre and Auguste, bought their own cellars. Having established their own house, they then bought one of the finest single vineyard sites in the whole of Champagne — the Clos des Goisses, 16 acres (5.5ha) of steep hillside that is planted with a mixture of Pinot Noir and Chardonnay.

For a period in the 1980s the house was linked to Gosset, but it was eventually acquired by the Marie Brizard Group, who then ran the marque in tandem with another house, Abel Lepitre, until November 1977. The company was then bought by Bruno Paillard on behalf of his Boizel Chanoine Champagne Group, after a deal with the workers' unions. The purchase included not only the Clos des Goisses but also Abel Lepitre, which is still made at the Reims cellars.

Clos des Goisses produces some of the finest and longest-lived champagnes, which are famed for their complexity of aroma and deep flavors. The company also produces a premium non-vintage blend called le Reflet, after the bottle-shaped reflection that the Clos leaves in the canal that runs alongside. This has 50% Pinot grapes from Goisses and the balance in Chardonnay from other vineyards. Non-vintage Brut and Rosé and vintage Brut and Blanc de Blancs make up the full selection.

the wines

champagne

Piper-Heidsieck

Owners: Rémy-Cointreau
Established: 1834
Located: Boulevard Henry Vasnier, Reims, France
Vineyards: 116 acres (47ha) within group
Sales: 6.5 million bottles
Exports: 50% or more
Deluxe Cuvées: Champagne Rare

Founded in 1834, the same year as Heidsieck & Co. and some years before Charles Heidsieck, the Piper brand remained independent until 1989 when it was united with Charles Heidsieck under the Rémy-Martin group.

The policy with Piper-Heidsieck is to produce wines that can be sold in a much larger volume than its Charles Heidsieck stablemate, without losing the house's identity or impairing the very fine quality. The wines are made under the supervision of Daniel Thibault and have evolved into a slightly fuller style than in years past. With all the work that has gone into reinforcing the quality of the company's other brands, it is not surprising that the Piper wines have developed so well.

The big brash campaign behind the recently repackaged non-vintage Brut, with its bright red label, is well supported by the company's reserve stocks. This is an excellent everyday champagne with good acidity and fruit. The non-dosage Brut Sauvage vintage wine is splendid champagne, bone-dry but not at all harsh or severe; the rosé Brut has a well-aged style and the prestige Champagne Rare an elegance that will develop further with a little bottle ageing.

the wines

champagne

Pommery

Owners: L.V.M.H.
Established: 1836
Located: Place du Général Gouraud, Reims, France
Vineyards: 758 acres (307ha)
Sales: Six million bottles
Exports: 70%
Deluxe Cuvées: Louise

The Pommery family was merely an investor in the champagne house of Greno, which owned Dubois-Gosset, until 1858 when, due to the level of its investment, the family took control when bad health forced Narcisse Greno to retire. Unfortunately, Louis Pommery died suddenly and his wife was forced to take the reins.

The widow Pommery then proceeded to become one of the great figures in 19th century champagne, with her development of dry wines and the linking of 11 miles (18km) of cellars which include 120 old Gallo-Roman chalk pits with many amazing bas-relief carvings. In 1879, her daughter married into the aristocratic Polignac family, which maintained control of the company up until 1979 when it was sold to Xavier Gardiner, who also owned Lanson. Since then the ownership has passed to LVMH, although Prince Alain de Polignac remains chef des caves.

The Moët policy for Pommery has obviously been one of boosting sales, which have doubled over the last 20 years. The main wine to have suffered is the basic Brut Royal, although this could also be because of the introduction of new wines — the Royal Arpanage, and the Summertime and Wintertime Cuvées. These are classic wines and must have been sourced from some of the finest blending material in the cellars. The deluxe cuvée, Louise, remains excellent quality with a crisp Chardonnay style and great finesse.

the wines

champagne

Louis Roederer

Owners: Champagne Louis Roederer
Established: Originally as Dubois Père & Fils, in 1760
Located: Boulevard Lundy, Reims, France
Vineyards: 470 acres (190ha)
Sales: 2.6 million bottles
Exports: 66%
Deluxe Cuvées: Cristal

One of the finest champagne producers, Roederer is one of the few houses which is almost self-sufficient in terms of grape supplies from the company's own vineyards. The family took control of the company in 1833, renaming it Louis Roederer, and proceeded to develop the Russian markets to such an extent that a personal request from Tsar Alexander II was the initiative for the production of the first bottles of Cristal, later to become one of the world's most sought after, and expensive, champagnes.

Another famous widow, Madame Olry-Roederer was responsible for running the company from the early 1930s for 40 years until she passed on control to her daughter and grandson Jean-Claude Rouzaud, who still manage the company.

The Brut Premier is a great focal point for the Roederer style, a full, fruity, body based on Pinot Noir, with soft oaky vanilla flavors from the well-aged reserve wines that are used in the blending, and a complex finish. The Brut vintage and Blanc de Blancs vintage have great depth and finesse, although I have been unlucky enough to have opened two oxidized bottles of the Blanc de Blancs in the last few years.

The famed Cristal, no longer the sweet wine made for the tsars, is an almost even split of Pinot Noir and Chardonnay, and can develop beautifully in bottle with great length and a dazzling finish.

the wines

champagne

Pol Roger

Owners: Champagne Pol Roger
Established: 1849
Located: Rue Henri Lalarge, Épernay, France
Vineyards: 210 acres (85 hectares
Sales: 1.3 million bottles
Exports: 65%
Deluxe Cuvées: Cuvée Sir Winston Churchill

Founded in 1849, and run for its first 50 years by Pol Roger, who started at the tender age of 19 years old, this is a house which is synonymous with family control — from wine production right through to marketing and sales. Pol Roger was succeeded by his sons Maurice and Georges, who in return added his Christian name to the surname of Roger to commemorate his achievements. Maurice Pol Roger, honorary life mayor of Épernay, continued the great work, and on his death control passed to his son Jacques, and then on to the great grandsons of the founder, Christian de Billy and Christian Pol Roger.

Until 1955 the company did not own vineyards but has since built up a sizeable estate. The non-vintage wines are an equal balance of Chardonnay, Pinot Noir, and Meunier, and show a delightful lightness of touch and delicate fruit. The vintage Blanc de Blancs and Rosé show distinct Chardonnay touches, and the Réserve Spéciale an extra level of depth. The Brut Vintage and Cuvée Sir Winston Churchill are truly great wines and age extremely well.

Pol Roger remains set in its ways: its aim is to produce the finest wines, each one chosen only by family members, and never to overextend the volume to the detriment of the reserve stocks required to ensure continuity.

the wines

champagne

Ruinart

Owners: L.V.M.H.
Established: 1729
Located: Rue des Crayères, 51100 Reims
Sales: Two million bottles
Exports: 23%
Deluxe Cuvées: Dom Ruinart

Ruinart, the oldest of all houses, was founded in 1729 to produce sparkling wines only from the Champagne region, by Nicolas Ruinart, who at that point was a very large cloth merchant in the region. Over the next 150 years four generations of the family were actively involved and the brand became well established in export markets, particularly Russia and the United States. The company remained family-controlled, albeit with additional funding from Baron Philippe de Rothschild in 1950, until 1963 when it was purchased by Moët & Chandon.

The standard cuvées, all under the R. de Ruinart badge, are rich and substantial wines with a Chardonnay influence running through them. The Dom Ruinart wines are a revelation, first produced at the end of the 1950s, and an undoubted success ever since. The Blanc de Blancs has rich vinous fruit and a complex mature biscuity finish and the Rosé has a similar base wine to the Blanc with the addition of very fine Pinot Noir.

One of the strangest things about the Ruinart wines is that they have never caught on in the same way that other great marques have. The insistence on top quality and a continued support of all things gastronomic have kept the brand firmly aimed at connoisseurs, and the wines offer really good value.

the wines

champagne

Seppelt Great Western

Owners: Southcorp Group
Established: 1851
Located: Great Western, Victoria, Australia
Vineyards: Almost uncountable acreage, in addition to a great deal of bought in grapes
Sales: Five million bottles
Exports: Less than 20%
Other Brands: Same group ownership as Seaview, an even larger producer

Almost since its arrival in Australia, the Seppelt family has been involved in wine production, and a good footing was provided by founder Joseph and his son Benno who were not shy in investing in large vineyard holdings. By the turn of the century they owned more than 1,500 acres (600ha) and had still to buy in 60% of the required grapes.

Seppelt's move into sparkling wines came with its purchase of the Great Western estate in 1918. After the installation of Colin Preece as winemaker the Great Western brand became the leading quality and value sparkling wine made in Australia. All of the Great Western wines are made from a large selection of grapes sourced mainly from Victoria and New South Wales.

The Vintage Harper's Pinot-Chardonnay and the Seppelt Pinot Chardonnay are big showy wines, not aimed for great ageing and the Blanc de Blancs Drumborg is made in very small batches. The stars of the show are the Salinger Vintage Brut, currently 1992, a wine that ages quite well but has a slightly blowsy feel to it, and the red Show Reserve Sparkling Shiraz, one of the world's biggest sparkling wines for body with huge berry flavors and concentration.

the wines

champagne

Taittinger

Owners: Taittinger Group
Established: As Fourneux in 1743 and Taittinger since 1932
Located: Place St. Nicaise, Reims, France
Vineyards: 642 acres (260ha)
Sales: Four million bottles
Exports: 60%
Other Brands: Irroy, St-Evremond

Unlike many of the other houses with long historical roots, Taittinger has only really come alive since World War II. The initial work done by Pierre Taittinger was enlarged upon by his sons, Claude, who is now chairman of the company, and François, who died in 1960. Taittinger, through application and acquisition, has become one of the largest companies in the area, and owns the house of Irroy, Bauvet in the Loire Valley, Domaine Carneros in California, and a host of industrial companies in hotels, construction and glassware.

Between the wars and during the expansion of the company, many quality vineyard sites were purchased, and these remain the core for today's cuvées. On recent tasting the Brut Réserve is a light, elegant, wine with a good mousse and a clean rich finish; the Brut Millésime has that little bit more depth and weight and the Rosé a rich, ripe, Pinot nose, and flavor.

The finest wines from the company are undoubtedly the Comtes de Champagne Cuvées, named in homage to Thibault IV, who back in the 1100s united the separate dukedoms of the region. The Taittinger family, proud owners of the ancestral home of the counts, have produced this cuvée since 1952 from highly rated vineyards in the Côtes des Blancs.

the wines

champagne

Further Reading

Michael Edwards; *The Champagne Companion*; Apple.

Patrick Forbes; *Champagne*; Gollancz.

Andrew Jefford; *The Magic of Champagne*; Webster's.

Hugh Johnson; *The World Atlas of Wine*; Mitchell Beazley.

Hugh Johnson; *Hugh Johnson's Wine Companion*; Mitchell Beazley.

Tom Stevenson; *World Encyclopedia of Champagne and sparkling wines*; Christie's.

Serena Sutcliffe (ed); *André Simon's Wines of the World*; Macdonald.